John Philip Newman

St. John - the Prisoner of Patmos

John Philip Newman

St. John - the Prisoner of Patmos

ISBN/EAN: 9783744758680

Printed in Europe, USA, Canada, Australia, Japan

Cover: Foto ©ninafisch / pixelio.de

More available books at **www.hansebooks.com**

ST. JOHN

THE PRISONER OF PATMOS

BY

BISHOP NEWMAN

NEW YORK
PRINTED BY HUNT & EATON
150 FIFTH AVENUE
1896

THIS MONOGRAPH

LOVINGLY INSCRIBED

TO OUR

DEAR FRIEND,

MRS. LELAND STANFORD.

PROLOGUE.

I VENTURE again to waft on a wavelet of Christian effort two more monographs from manuscripts presented to me by Bishop Newman for the Evangel Systematized Perpetual Bible Readers' Fund.

The first of these booklets is entitled *St. John, the Prisoner of Patmos*, from a recent visit to this sacred island. Its companion is entitled *Aurora Borealis Amid the Icebergs of Greenland's Mountains*, written while at this northernmost part of our hemisphere.

We trust they will be crowned with the same favor as their predecessors, *The White Stone* and *Pearl of Pearls*, and bring into the Bible treasury as many silver dollars.

This formulated perpetual fund was adopted and legalized by the Woman's Foreign Missionary Society of the Methodist Episcopal Church at its recent executive session at St. Louis. Already six native Bible women are reading under this plan.

MRS. J. P. NEWMAN.

ST. JOHN,

THE PRISONER OF PATMOS.

S T. JOHN touched three centuries. Born in the last lustrum of the last century B. C., he lived through the first one hundred years of the Christian era and closed his eventful career at Ephesus in the reign of Trajan at the beginning of the second century. He outlived twelve Roman emperors, inclusive of Augustus and Nerva, two of whom committed suicide, seven of whom were murdered, and nearly all of whom were the merciless persecutors of the religion which is now the hope and joy of humanity. All the holy apostles had been crowned with martyrdom, and he was left to settle the canon of the Gospel history by formally attesting the truth of the first three gospels and writing his own to supply what they left wanting.

He was born under the magnificent reign of Cæsar Augustus, whose vast empire swept from the River Euphrates to the Western Ocean, and from the Wall of Antoninus to the Mountains of the Moon, and within whose vast empire dwelt one hundred and twenty millions of our race. Of the splendor of that age it is difficult to speak in adequate terms. All that wealth could procure, or genius create, or ambition desire, filled Rome with glory and the provincial capitals with temples and palaces. It was an age of renown. Poets and orators, statesmen and warriors, philosophers and historians added greatness to the period, while luxury and vice, war and conquest, prodigality and meanness held high carnival.

In a small province of that great empire, and on the peaceful shores of Gennesaret, St. John was born. His father had accumulated wealth from the fisheries of his native lake, and his son passed frequently from Tiberias to Jerusalem in the management of his father's business. There is a well-founded tradition that Zebedee had a city residence in Jerusalem, which he sold to the high priest Caiaphas, and which accounts for the consideration that Caiaphas extended to St. John on the night of our Lord's trial.

It is an old saying that great men have great mothers. St. John's mother was Salome, sister of the Virgin Mary, who was St. John's aunt, and he was first cousin to our Lord. She was a positive, decided, ambitious woman, who desired that her two sons should have the most conspicuous positions in the Messiah's coming kingdom, of which she fondly dreamed. Her comparative wealth permitted her to follow the Lord and minister to his wants in all his journeyings. She was at the cross. She purchased the spices for the Lord's burial, and she was among the first at the tomb in the morning of the resurrection, when she saw the Lord. Some pronounced her a managing, ambitious mother, like Rebecca of old, because she coveted exalted positions for her sons; but her petition was a compliment to her faith in the on-coming glory of the Messiah's kingdom. Excited by the popular acclaim at that moment accorded to the Christ, which to her was the promise of the Messiah's larger glory in the future, she based her claim on family relationship, and requested that her sons, cousins-german to our Lord, should be exalted with him in his glory. And her sons were exalted. Her son James was the first of the apostles to wear the martyr's crown, and her son, the beloved John, is revered wherever Christ is known. If her sister Mary is " blessed among women " as the mother of Jesus, Salome is the mother of him "whom Jesus loved." She is one of the great mothers in the annals of our race, and as the mother of a great son she ranks with Susanna Wesley and Mary Washington.

In all the ages and in all lands men have esteemed it the highest honor to be the intimate friend of a great man. Kings, statesmen, and scholars have had their favorites, to whom they confided their inmost thoughts and disclosed their projecting plans. Christ had many disciples, seventy evangelists, and twelve apostles. Out of the illustrious twelve he selected three to be his confidential companions, and of the three he chose St. John, who has the rare preeminence of being "the disciple whom Jesus loved."

Why this honor? His personal beauty? All the artists, ancient and modern, whether they wrought on marble or on canvas, conceived of him as the perfection of manly beauty, who charmed all by the gracefulness of his proportions and the sweetness of his manners. Was it the repose and clearness of his intellect? All his reported utterances and all his writings indicate a high order of mind. His letters to the " elect lady" are the purest and sweetest in literature; his gospel is the most incisive, analytical, and subjective transmitted to us; his Apocalypse is sublime in imagery, grand in diction, and powerful in description of all the sacred books. In all literature there is nothing more beautiful than his story of Bethany, nothing more pathetic than his " Mary to the Saviour's tomb," and his pen portraiture of Christ as he appeared to him on Patmos is as fault- less as it is majestic. Shall we not rather say it was his Christian character assimilated into the likeness of Christ?

What a miracle of grace was St. John! Born amid the mountains of Galilee and on the oft-swept storm shores of his native Tiberias, his impetuous spirit had been christened "Son of Thunder." His vehement temper would blaze forth like a mountain on fire, and in his im- pulsive vindictiveness he would call down fire from heaven on the offending villagers of Samaria. By nature a bigot, he preferred that a demon should for- ever torment a brother man than to have the evil spirit expelled by an unknown disciple of his Lord. Grace changed all this. His strong spirit became calm as the embosomed Lake of Gennesaret when peaceful zephyrs whispered o'er its tranquil bosom. The bigot became the generous friend of all men, and the vindictive disciple became the apostle of love.

Who occupies a more conspicuous place in New Testament history than St. John? But we should go to an earlier period than the baptism of Jesus for the origin of this intimacy. As Mary and Salome were sisters and Elizabeth was their cousin, and as these three mothers were devout Jewesses, it is more than probable that in their youths Jesus and St. John and John the Baptist often met in Jerusalem at the great

national feasts whither their parents
went. Having received their elementary
education in their native towns, and as
Jewish lads were sent at the age of
twelve to one of the many colleges in
Jerusalem, it is highly probable that
they were at college together, and for
aught we know in the school of Gamaliel,
where they met young Saul of Tarsus.
What a group for a painter! Christ,
the Saviour ; John the Baptist, the fore-
runner; St. John, the evangelist ; and
St. Paul, the apostle to the whole Gen-
tile world.   Did they ever talk of their
future ?

St. John was an early disciple of John
the Baptist, and in his gospel he de-
votes to him thirty-seven verses of a
chapter of fifty-one verses. He wit-

nessed the baptism of Jesus, and recorded the testimony of the great baptizer. He was the unnamed disciple who stood with the baptizer and St. Andrew. His own record of the Christ, written more than fifty years thereafter, is too beautiful to omit: "Again the next day after, John stood, and two of his disciples; and looking upon Jesus as he walked, he saith, Behold the Lamb of God! And the two disciples heard him speak, and they followed Jesus. Then Jesus turned, and saw them following, and saith unto them, What seek ye? And they said unto him, Master, where dwellest thou? He saith unto them, Come and see. They came and saw where he dwelt, and abode with him that day: for it was about the tenth

2

hour. One of the disciples which heard
John speak, and followed him, was
Andrew, Simon Peter's brother." What
a memorable night was that! Could
they ever forget it?

And now for three years, in the heat
of summer and the cold of winter, in
journeyings oft from Capernaum to Jerusalem, through the hamlets of Galilee,
Samaria, and Judea, on Tabor and
Olivet, on the peaceful lake and on the
stormy sea, in the solitude of the desert
and the crowded metropolis, when trav-
eling with the twelve and surrounded
with thronging multitudes, by day and
by night, St. John was the constant,
intimate, confiding companion of the
world's Messiah. He saw him walk on
the Sea of Galilee and transfigured on

Mount Tabor, and heard him call to life again the damsel of Capernaum, the widow's son of Nain, and Lazarus of Bethany. He saw Mary of Magdala restored to virtue, blind Bartimeus receive his sight, and Simon the leper cleansed. He heard the wonderful discourses of the Christ, listened to his sacerdotal prayers, and witnessed the terrible onslaughts of Pharisee and Sadducee in fierce controversy. He sat with him on the slopes of Olivet when he wept over the doomed Jerusalem and foretold the destruction of that far-famed city. He joined the joyful procession when Jesus entered Jerusalem in triumph. He was at the last supper, and was present in the garden of agony. He boldly stood by the side of his Master in the palace

of Caiaphas, and was with him through
that long and dreadful night when in the
hands of the mob.   He was last at the
cross and received the dying glance of
the world's Redeemer, and was early at
the empty tomb and was the first to believe in the Lord's resurrection.   His
keen, far-sighted vision was the first to
discern the Lord standing on the distant shores of Tiberias, commanding his
friends to " cast the net on the right
side of the ship."   With the " eleven "
and a great company of disciples, both
men and women, he saw the ascending
Christ pass into the heavens of love.
No wonder that in his first general
epistle he could say, " That which was
from the beginning, which we have
heard, which we have seen with our

eyes, which we have looked upon, and our hands have handled, of the Word of life, declare we unto you."

Less than forty years of his life are now behind him ; more than sixty years stretch out before him.   And what momentous years !   He is detained in Jerusalem to comfort and care for Mary, the mother of our Lord.   We catch only glimpses of him during less than half the period.   He confronts the magician, Simon Magus, in Samaria ; he heals with Peter a cripple at the "Gate Beautiful" in the Holy City, and with him is sent to prison ; and in the year 50 A. D. he is present in the first great Christian council, held in Jerusalem, and listens to Paul pleading the Christian rights of the heathen world.

From all that we can learn from Scripture and infer from tradition, St. John was resident of Jerusalem more than thirty years, from the ascension of the Lord till the death of Mary. He was her provider and guardian, and it is more than probable that her home was the headquarters of the Christians of Jerusalem and of all who came from afar to visit the scenes forever memorable in the history of Christ. " Blessed among women," her gentle, submissive, obedient spirit was an inspiration to all the saints. How earnestly they gathered around her while she recited the life story of her divine Son, her own maiden life, her espousal to the good Joseph, the visit to her of the angel Gabriel, her visit to her cousin Elizabeth, that toilsome journey to Beth-

lehem to be enrolled and taxed, the birth
of her Son, the song of the angels, the
coming of the shepherds, the "Star of
the East," the visit of the "Wise Men,"
the slaughter of the innocents, her flight
into Egypt, her return to Nazareth, the
finding of her missing Son in the temple
with the doctors, the eighteen years of
sweet domestic life amid the hills of her
Nazarene home, and the departure of her
Son, when he bade farewell to his mother
and the scenes of his childhood to enter
upon that public ministry wherewith to
bless mankind. And how equally thrilling
must have been her recital of all she had
felt and heard and seen throughout those
three great years, from the wedding in
Cana to the crucifixion on Calvary, and
from the empty tomb of Joseph of Ari-

mathea to the ascension from Olivet. It
is reasonable to believe that she lived
to the advanced age of eighty years and
was permitted to die in peace. Neither
Herod nor Nero was suffered to molest
her, and while the storm of persecution
raged with unwonted fury around her,
and her nephew, James, was beheaded
with the sword and St. Peter was imprisoned, the angels protected her until
commanded to escort her to the pres-
ence of her glorified Son. And what a
funeral was hers when all the " followers
of the Lamb," led by St. John as chief
mourner, conveyed her precious remains
out of St. Stephen's Gate, across the
Valley of the Kidron, to a spot near the
Garden of Gethsemane, where is the tra-
ditional tomb, the shrine which to this

day attracts pilgrims and travelers to the " City of the Great King."

St. John is now free to leave forever the Holy City. Nero is Emperor of Rome. Herod Agrippa I rules all Palestine. Premonitions of the coming storm of woe and death were apparent to all. Herod had killed St. James, beloved brother of St. John, and had imprisoned St. Peter to put him to death. The Jews were restless under the oppressions of the Romans. Nero had appointed to the governorship of Palestine Gessius Florus, that systematic plunderer of the people, who were provoked to rise in their last rebellion. Vespasian, with sixty thousand soldiers, had subdued all Palestine except Jerusalem. The Christians prepared to leave the

Holy City and seek refuge in Pella, sixty
miles from Jerusalem, overlooking the
Jordan, amid the mountains of Gilead.
The news came that Nero had beheaded
St. Paul in Rome, and the "Seven
Churches of Asia" were left without a
leader. St. John discerns the signs of
the times as the " beginning of sorrows,"
and recalls his Master's words, " Let
them which be in Judea flee unto the
mountains." When the last of the Christians had escaped, St. John takes a farewell view of Jerusalem. Once more and
for the last time he visits Gethsemane
and Calvary, the empty tomb and the
Mount of Ascension, the temple where
the Saviour had so often taught, and the
scene of Pentecost; then, lingering to
offer a prayer where St. Stephen was

stoned and St. James was beheaded and
James the Less was murdered, and where
the blessed Mary was buried, he ascends
the heights of Scopus and takes his last
view of the doomed city. How magnificent the scene—that great city four
and a half miles in circuit, with walls
forty feet high, protected by one hundred
and ninety towers, with Hippicus and
Phasaelus and Mariamne and Psephinos
rising to the height of one hundred and
fifty feet, with the white marble palace
of Herod on Mount Zion and the Holy
Temple on Mount Moriah, with its courts
and galleries and porticos, its Beautiful
Gate, and protected by the massive
Tower of Antonia, wherein was Pilate's
Judgment Hall! As he stood there in
sad meditation he could hear the tramp

of Titus and his legions as they came from Egypt, from Cæsarea, and from Tiberias, to encamp on the very hill whereon he now stood. What a prophetic vision rose before him of the terrible onset of war and famine, of pestilence and conflagration, when the flames of the Holy Temple should redden those Syrian skies, amid the groans of the dying and the imprecations of the fallen!

Henceforth St. John is an exile. He is for the first time on the "Great Sea" —the tideless Mediterranean, "whose shores are empires." As he advances, his native land recedes from view and the snows of Hermon are seen for the last time. Never again will he sail on his native Gennesaret or tread the

streets of Jerusalem.   All those dear to
his heart's best love have passed away,
and he is a traveler in a new country.
Before his prophetic soul pass in solemn
review   the   calamities   soon   to   come
upon the " Land of Promise," the por-
tents of which are already apparent.
But great thoughts of the future of his
Master's kingdom arouse him from his
sad reveries.   Day after day he sails
over the blue waters of the mighty deep,
and new scenes allure him on.   On his
right is Tarsus, where Paul was born; on
his left is Cyprus, home of Barnabas, the
" Son   of   Consolation."   Now   he   sees
Rhodes and the Colossus that spanned
the entrance to the harbor, and soon he
enters the mole of Miletus, the port of
Ephesus, his future home.

Whether it was the dying request of
St. Paul or the special petition of the
elders that St. John should reside
among the "seven churches of Asia,"
one thing is clear, that Ephesus is to be
to him in the future what Jerusalem has
been in the memorable past. He went
from one capital to another, where men
do most congregate, where power is
centralized, and whence issue far-reach-
ing and commanding influences. He is
now in the glorious city of Ephesus, the
most renowned in Ionic Asia. From
Crœsus to Constantine, for one thousand
years, it had stood in its glory. It owed
its greatness to Lysimachus, successor of
Alexander the Great. Its chief renown
was the Temple of Diana, whose fame
had filled the world. What Minerva

was to the Athenians, Diana was to the Ephesians. Such was the adoration paid to the goddess that all Greek cities contributed to the magnificence of her shrine. On the night that Alexander the Great was born that splendid fane was destroyed by fire. All Greece responded to the call of her worshipers, and Diana of the Ephesians was enshrined in greater glory. Kings gave their crowns and women their jewels. Out of the white marble from Mount Prion was formed its noble colonnade, four hundred and twenty-five feet long and two hundred and twenty feet wide, of columns sixty feet high and six feet in diameter, each one the gift of a king. Of the temple itself it is impossible to speak in terms of adequate grandeur.

Within the shrine was the image of the goddess which superstition claimed had fallen from the skies, and within was deposited the wealth of western Asia, so that the temple was to the Ephesians what the Bank of England is to Great Britain. Associated therewith was the power of magic, expressed in monograms on amulets, to charm away evil spirits, and on which those books were written which, under the mighty preaching of St. Paul, were committed to the flames, but which act excited the mob to the wildest frenzy, whose shout was, "Great is Diana of the Ephesians!"

This was the proud, wealthy, superstitious city, the future home of St. John. Paul and Apollos, Aquila and

Priscilla were not there to greet him, but the " elders of Ephesus " were there to receive him, the last remaining of the holy apostles.   But his stay was brief. The Neronian persecution broke forth with malignant fury.   The Emperor Claudius was dead, and Nero was on the throne of the Cæsars, who was permitted to reign through fourteen years, the darkest in all the bloody history of the twelve Cæsars, whose memories are recalled with horror.   This sixth Cæsar was " born for a curse to virtue and mankind, and all earth cannot show so black a mind." The ghosts of his mother, Agrippina, and of his wife, Octavia, and of Seneca, his teacher, and Lucan, the poet, and Britannicus, the son of Claudius, all of whom he mur-

3

dered, will ever "sit heavy on his soul."
He tortured the Roman Christians by
the most inhuman methods, and sen-
tenced St. Paul to martyrdom. His
persecutions swept to the utmost prov-
inces of his empire, and neither youth
nor beauty nor sex escaped the madness
of his rage. St. John was too conspicuous in station and character to go un-
noticed. He was arrested and carried
to Rome to stand trial before this mon-
ster of history, who condemned him to
be thrown into a caldron of boiling oil;
but, escaping unhurt, the tyrant banished
him to Patmos. When on his voyage
to Ephesus he must have sighted this
now famous island, but little did he
then reck that it would be his prison
home for many years.

At that time the islands of the Levant were densely populated, and the Ægean Sea was white with the sails of many vessels. In our recent visit to Patmos we saw much of these Grecian islands forever famous in the history of the world. We had spent the day at Syra, the ancient Syros of the Cyclades, ten miles long and five miles wide, where dwell thirty-four thousand people of the Greek and Latin faith. Its capital, Hermopolis, is a busy town of twenty-one thousand seamen and merchants, in whose harbor float the flags of many nations. It is a white city, whose lofty hill is crowned with the noble Church of St. George. Here was born Pherecydes, tutor of Pythagoras, and hither came the refugees from all parts of Greece

during the war of the revolution. It
was nine o'clock at night when we embarked on our little steamer of twenty-
five tons, called the *John Maxwell*. Our
proposed voyage had excited the town,
and crowds of Syrians followed us in
groups and wondered at our going. Our
small craft was chartered for the occa-
sion and was manned by seven Greek
sailors. It seemed a bold venture of
faith in God and trust in human nature
to go alone with these unknown seamen
on a night voyage of eighty miles and on
a sea subject to severe and sudden
storms; but to stand on Patmos allayed
all fears and inspired the necessary cour-
age. Twice we had seen the " Sacred
Isle " from the deck of the passenger
steamer when we were *en route* from

Jerusalem to Athens and Constantinople, but it was a privilege we could not now forego to traverse the valleys and ascend the mountains on that island whither St. John was banished for the "word of God and for the testimony of Jesus Christ." My only companion on that midnight voyage was the "wife of my youth," who with me had traveled the "wide world over."

It is more than probable that, on his return voyage from Rome, St. John reached his prison island over the Ionian Sea, through the Gulf of Patras, up the Gulf of Corinth, and, disembarking to cross the isthmus, he again embarked at Salamis, and thence sailed amid these same islands which now met our gaze. Then the culture of Greece and the

wealth of Rome had covered these islands with sacred shrines and temples
of renown, and, as his prophetic eye
glanced down the coming centuries, his
great soul must have rejoiced in pros-
pect that the divine Master whose prisoner he was would some day reign over
all the Ægean Sea.

All night long we sailed over these
same waters and recalled the history of
these same islands. The sea was calm,
the sky cloudless, the starlight bril-
liant, the moon full. There on our left
was Tenos, home of the old Ionians, who
were compelled to serve in the fleets of
Xerxes in the naval battle of Salamis.
Not more than sixty miles in circumfer-
ence, its outline appeared to the beholder
a long, lofty chain of hills. Here lived

in wealth and luxury the old Venetian merchants, and it is now the summer resort of wealthy Ægeans who love the wines of Tenos. An hour later we sailed along the silent shores of Delos, toward which the eyes of all Greece turned to its holy shrines. The birthplace of Apollo and Artemis, it was the sanctuary of the Ægean, whose oracle, enshrined in the Temple of Apollo, rivaled that of Delphi in sanctity, and thither Spartan and Athenian came to pay their homage and offer their gifts. What scenes of mirth once occurred on these now silent shores, when the "Ionians, in their long flowing robes,. danced to the music of lute and pipe in the shade of the sacred palm;" when poets recited and athletes contended; when kings and warriors were banqueted at public expense! All now is changed : the night winds sighed through the broken arches of blue marble ; the grand Portico of Philip is gone ; the white marble Temple of Apollo is a ruin ; the famous oracle of Delos is as silent as a tomb, and the cultured paganism of Greece has been superseded by temples dedicated to the Christ of St. John.

Far into the night we had on our right Oliaros, Paros, and Naxos, three immortal islands, memorable for the great deeds of great men. In the white grotto of Oliaros is that wonderful chamber, one hundred by one hundred and fifty feet, from whose ceiling depend those snow-white stalactites twenty-five feet long. As we passed the head of a nar-

row strait we saw the round mountain of
Paros, sloping evenly down to the plain
which surrounds it; it is Mount Mar-
pessa, containing the quarries of Parian
marble out of which were sculptured the
Medicean "Venus" and the "Dying Glad-
iator," and out of which came the marble
for the tomb of Napoleon, under the
dome of the Hôtel des Invalides. And
here Darius planted his banners after the
battle of Marathon, and here Miltiades
received his death wound when he sought
to reconquer the island. Unmindful of
such historic scenes, the shepherd of to-
day wanders with his flocks of sheep and
goats over the mountain slopes. How
splendidly Paros stood out in the moonlight of that memorable night, covered
with many dwellings with their terraced

roofs rising from out beautiful gardens;
and most conspicuous of all the scene
was the Church of "Our Lady of the
Hundred Gates," attributed to Helena,
mother of Constantine the Great. Far
away to the eastward appeared the re-
volving light on Cape Psilos, on the great
island of Naxos, the most fertile and
beautiful of the archipelago, twelve miles
wide and ten miles long, the abode
of twenty thousand Greek and Latin
Christians. How weird appeared in the
moonlight their white houses, whose
sleeping inmates dreamed not that the
eyes of a stranger were gazing on their
silent homes. No wonder that the
Greeks dedicated this island to Bacchus,
whose wines rival the best in the Levant,
and whose groves of the olive, orange,

lemon, fig, and pomegranate give wealth
to the owner and pleasure to the traveler. Looking over the calm sea to the
northeast, we saw the strong light on
the great island of Icaria, scene of that
legend of Icarus, whose wings of feathers
and wax melted in the sun when he
mounted too high in his flight from
Minos, and, falling, was drowned near
this historic island.

The night was now far spent; we ceased
our vigils, and in our sleep dreamed of
Patmos. At four the next morning we
came again on the deck of our little
steamer. Aurora, with her rosy fingers,
was lifting the curtains of the dawn; the
moon had disappeared, and the stars one
by one had faded from our view. So
placid were the waters that we seemed

to be gliding over a sea of glass; a gentle
breeze came whispering o'er the deep;
the pilot was at the wheel, and naught
was heard save the steady stroke of the
engine. Soon the bold, cliffy outlines of
the long-wished-for island came in view.
It was sunrise on Patmos. What memories were awakened, what emotions were
inspired! The past returned with the
actualities of the present. The visions
of the Apocalypse were seen in the ver-
ities of history. Nero the tyrant, St.
John the exile—emperor and apostle,
persecutor and persecuted—were in imagination alive again.

Situated in the Ægean, south from
Smyrna, and less than twenty miles from
the mainland of Asia Minor, the island
of Patmos is ten miles long, five miles

wide, and less than thirty in circuit. A narrow isthmus divides the island into almost equal parts north and south, with Port Scala on the east and Port Merika on the west. On this narrow strip of land stood the ancient city in whose harbor St. John landed. The whole coast is deeply indented; the lofty cliffs rise out of the sea; the valleys are deep and solemn; the mountains attain an altitude of one thousand feet, from whose summits is obtained a magnificent view of sea and bay, of islet and island, of vale and craggy height. Here and there palm and olive, fig and mulberry, cypress and oak, almond and pine adorn the island and give industry to the people. Five thousand souls dwell there in peace, industrious and thrifty. Order reigns, and one policeman is the guardian of life and property. Patmos is one of the " Fortunate Isles." No Turk has trodden its soil, no mosque shadows its landscape ; the small government tax of two thousand five hundred dollars is annually carried by a deputy to the pasha of Rhodes. Neither piracy nor slavery nor the plague has ever cursed its shores. The islanders are Greek Christians, gentle, intelligent, happy, and in its clear, pure atmosphere dwell together as brethren. As we passed through their streets and along their highways they opened their doors and greeted us with flowers and saluted us with genuine hospitality.

From early dawn to our arrival the bold and massive southwestern cliffs of

Patmos, like some Cyclopean wall rising
from the sea, appeared to view, and over
against the dark background a solitary
sail was seen white in the morning light,
moving slowly in the light breeze toward
some neighboring island.   The approach
was enchanting; hour after hour, in the
stillness of the morning, we drew nearer
and nearer; the illusion of nearness was
fascinating yet deceptive.   Winds and
waves had indented the rock-bound coast
and carved out many a grotto which re-
sounded to the voice of the deep.   Far
away, one thousand feet above us, was
seen Mount Elias, crowned with a temple to the prophet.   Soon the white city
appeared on the distant hills, clustering
around the " Monastery of St. John the
Divine."   Now we entered the quiet har-

bor of La Scala, landlocked, not unlike
two thirds of a circle, and wherein were
ships at anchor. The village of La Scala,
the Lower Town, and the principal port
of the island, is on the eastern side of
the isthmus, on the shores of a quiet little bay, wherein one third of the people
reside, mostly merchants who trade in
fruits. The Upper Town is on a lofty
hill, half an hour's ride up a steep road,
paved with large round stones hard to
the foot of man and beast. We were
en route for the Monastery of St. John.
Our coming had been announced, and at
the gate of the monastery the venerable
bishop and his forty monks received us
with much ceremony and many cordial
greetings. Each wore the black robe
and brimless hat peculiar to Greek

monks.   They conducted us to the ca-
thedral, not unlike in ornamentation the
Greek churches we had seen in Russia.
Then we were escorted to the reception
chamber, adjoining which was the room
where we were to lodge, and wherein we
conversed for hours on the progress of
Christianity in the East and in the West.

For one thousand years the monks of
the Order of St. Christodulus have occu-
pied Patmos, the gift of the Emperor
Alexis I, sometimes called Comnenus,
who in the eleventh century issued a
golden bull, which is still preserved,
granting this island to them to found
thereon a monastery, which is the origin
of the " Monastery of St. John the Divine."   Theirs is now one of the richest
monastic orders in the East, and to it
4

belongs the southern half of the island, with possessions in Samos, Crete, and other islands of the Levant. We found the monks of Patmos refined and intelligent, and we saw one whose saintly face and gentle manners reminded us of the " Beloved Disciple." They elect out of their number one to be their bishop, who reports to the Patriarch of Constantinople. Fifty years ago they had here a flourishing school of languages, attended by many students from neighboring islands and from distant lands, but now they teach in the village schools and devote themselves to study and meditation.

Our visit to the library was replete with interest. Of the six hundred ancient manuscripts once here about three hundred remain, some of which are of high antiquity and of great value. The one of most absorbing interest to us is the story of the life of St. John from the ascension of our Lord to his release from exile, said to have been written by one of St. John's personal friends, and with it we found the monks quite familiar. From the library we passed through the cloisters and cells and chapels of the old monastery, which crowns one of the highest hills, and which, with its massive walls, towers, and battlements, resembles a fortress. Ascending to the highest terrace, we had an entrancing view of a panorama never to be forgotten, and in the clear atmosphere could be seen Icaria, Naxos, and numberless islets resting on the calm bosom of the Ægean. Descending to the

lower galleries, we passed out to visit the
Convent of the Holy Sisters, wherein are
forty nuns of the Greek Church, most of
them aged ; one is blind, one is noted as
a linguist, all are devoted to sweet char-
ity, and all live in peace.

Guided by Brother Mucarius, a gentle
spirit, we came down the mountain to
the Church of the Holy Grotto, the tra-
ditional prison of St. John, where Mucarius is the parish priest, and who be-
lieves the legends he recites to others.
The little church is built over what
seems to be a natural grotto. In the
steep hillside is the recess in the rock
wherein the head of the illustrious exile
rested when asleep, and above it is the
sign of the Greek cross he made in the
rock. Over the altar is a picture of St.

John in a heavenly trance, to whom
Christ appears in glory with saints and
angels. While to us this grotto was im-
pressive, we preferred to think of him as
having the freedom of the island, and
when threading its solemn valleys or
standing on its majestic mountains
Christ appeared to him in those marvelous visions of "the things which thou
hast seen, and the things which are, and
the things which shall be hereafter."

The monks of Patmos are in accord
with the current tradition that St. John
was banished to the island during the
Neronian persecution, which continued
four years, from A. D. 64 to 68 ; but how
long he remained is an unsettled ques-
tion. There is no indication that Nero,
a heartless tyrant, would cease his cruel-

ties on the Christians during his reign,
nor is there a suspicion of hope that during the brief and tumultuous reigns of
the vicious Galba, Otho, and Vitellius,
whose imperial lives covered less than a
year, any attention would be given to
relieve the persecuted disciples of the
Lord. Vespasian, who succeeded these
" Mock Emperors," and who reigned for
ten years, from A. D. 69 to 79, and who
is considered wise and beneficent, the
patron of science and art, may have sus-
pended the cruelties practiced on the
Christians, but there is nothing in history to suggest that he was tolerant toward Christianity. There is more ground
for hope that St. John was released from
exile by the Emperor Titus, who succeeded his father Vespasian in A. D. 79,

whose wisdom and kindness won for him the honorable title, " The Delight of Mankind." The Jews had compelled him by their madness to destroy the Holy Temple when he took Jerusalem, and that against his protest ; and this his noble protest was in harmony with his public sympathy for his people, as shown in his visit to the distressed districts laid waste by the eruption of Vesuvius, when Pompeii and Herculaneum were destroyed. Whether the apostle's banishment lasted ten years or fifteen, there is a prevalent opinion, which seems well founded, that St. John wrote the Apocalypse while in exile, and on his return to Ephesus he finished his gospel at the age of eighty, and penned his epistles in his ninetieth year.

As we read the Book of Revelation
on the scene of its wonderful manifesta-
tions, we were impressed with the sim-
plicity and nobility of St. John's own
statement of his imprisonment : "I John,
who also am your brother, and companion in tribulation, and in the kingdom and
patience of Jesus Christ, was in the isle
that is called Patmos, for the word of God,
and for the testimony of Jesus Christ."
How simple and exalted the record! He
is a " companion in tribulation ; " he
omits the circumstances of his arrest, the
time, the place, the emperor, but states
the fact and the island of his banishment, and that without comment.
He omits all that exalts self, all those
personal allusions which fill the biographies of great men, all the daily incidents

of those he met, what he saw, and how he passed those dreary years of confinement away from the society and fellowship of believers; yet in all he writes there is not one word of complaint.

My Lord, how full of sweet content,
I pass my years of banishment !
Where'er I dwell, I dwell with thee,
In heaven, in earth, or on the sea.
To me remains nor place nor time ;
My country is in every clime :
I can be calm and free from care
On any shore, since God is there.

While place we seek, or place we shun,
The soul finds happiness in none ;
But with a God to guide our way,
'Tis equal joy, to go or stay.
Could I be cast where thou art not,
That were indeed a dreadful lot ;
But regions none remote I call,
Secure of finding God in all.

—*Madame Guyon.*

He is careful to designate to whom he writes, and who were to be custodians of the wonderful book; he addresses his message to the " seven churches of Asia." And there were but " seven ; " there had been eight, but in the ninth year of Nero's reign an earthquake overwhelmed both Laodicea and Colossæ, which were not far apart, and when Laodicea was rebuilt Colossæ remained a ruin, and its church became identified with that of the Laodiceans. During his absence grave errors had been received, and to correct them and destroy their influence he writes like one familiar with the facts.

Having warned those in error and cheered those who were steadfast, great thoughts now fill his mind and mighty visions pass before his prophetic view. He hears a voice saying, " Come up hither, and I will show thee things which must be hereafter." He is called to make a record which should be to the Church for all time, a perpetual prophet, always speaking of successive events and their fulfillment as ages roll on, which seems to be the design of the Apocalypse, that book of wonders. To St. John was revealed the fall of empires, the downfall of tyrants, and the overthrow of all opposing powers. The trumpets sounded ; the vials of woes were emptied ; the seals of mysteries were broken ; the day of calamities had come. Nero was burning the Christians, like so many torches, to light up his royal gardens in Rome. He had slain

St. Paul at Tre Fontane. Throughout
the empire his minions of woe were
burning or beheading or casting to the
wild beasts of the arena men, women,
and children whose only offense was
their faith in Christ. What shall be the
final issue? Martyrs must be supported
by the promise of ultimate triumph, the
faith of survivors must be cheered to en-
dure cruel mockings. Who shall con-
quer in the end, Christ or Cæsar? The
Church must be assured that all opposition to the Church of the Lord shall go
down forever. This is the mission of the
Apocalypse.

We are without information how long
the apostle was in writing his book
called " The Revelation of Jesus Christ ;"
whether it was a rapid, continuous effort,

or written at long intervals during his stay upon the island ; whether he wrote at the time when some of the national events occurred, or antecedent or subsequent thereto.   Twelve times he is commanded to " write ; " sometimes the thought and language are his own, anon both are dictated to him.   He was " in the Spirit," under divine influence to guide and suggest, and it was on the " Lord's day "—the Christian Sabbath. These revelations came to him from those who appeared to him from out the unseen world, who dictated to him what he wrote ; he saw much in vision, either by illumination of imagination or by pictorial representation of passing events, and of the things that were to come to pass in the far distant future of our world's history, and evidently much came to him by suggestion and impulse; but whether the one or the other, he was "in the Spirit on the Lord's day." As by a series of dissolving views he presents to the Church the fall of the Roman empire; the destruction of Jerusalem and the final overthrow of the Jewish commonwealth, the rise and fall of papal Rome under the figure of the " scarlet woman ; " the origin and spread of Mohammedanism—the " false prophet; " the dawn and increasing splendor of the Reformation ; and the final triumph of Messiah's reign, when shall appear " a new heaven and a new earth : for the first heaven and the first earth were passed away."

Much of the bold imagery wherewith

St. John clothed his thoughts may have
been suggested by the surrounding
landscape of his island home. Looking
out from some mountain peak into the
boundless expanse before him, he saw " a
throne set in the heaven ; " there are
times when the roar of the mighty Ægean
is as " the sound of many waters ; " so
profound is the calm sometimes there
that the ocean is like unto a " sea of glass
like unto crystal ; " in the dawn and at
sunset, when falls the golden light of the
sun on the still waters, the scene resembles a " sea of glass mingled with fire ; "
and when the war of the elements is on,
when sea, air, and sky are in commotion,
when lightnings flash and thunder
answers thunder, when the Euroclydon
blows from Mount Ida, and all nature

seems in her last convulsions, then " every mountain and island were moved out of their places, and every island fled away, and the mountains were not found."

In all this marvelous book there is nothing more interesting and consoling to the human heart than Christ's personal and visible appearance to his friend, and that after the lapse of thirty-five years. A year after the ascension St. Stephen saw the Lord; three years thereafter St. Paul conversed with him on the way to Damascus; and now St. John beholds him face to face, looks upon that familiar and glorified form, and once more hears that voice that had so often stirred his inmost soul: " I am he that liveth, and was dead; and, behold, I am alive for evermore." This is the sweetest and most assuring of all the New Testament epiphanies, and when we read it where it had occurred it filled our souls with hope and joy unspeakable and full of glory, as the unanswerable argument of our immortality and the crowning proof that our departed friends still live, and sometimes come to us to cheer us in our struggle for the crown of life.

And St. John is favored with two views of our Lord, one as he will ever appear to his friends—in his personality— and another in his official dignity. How sublime the contrast! He says: " I was in the Spirit on the Lord's day "—which was to emphasize the resurrection of Christ—" and heard behind me a great

5

voice, as of a trumpet "—a call from afar
of majesty and strength, filling all the
air for a wide distance, announcing a
fact : " I am Alpha and Omega, the first
and the last." Then followed the glorious vision : " I saw seven golden candlesticks; and in the midst of the seven
candlesticks one like unto the Son of
man "—the chosen appellation of himself—" clothed with a garment down to
the foot "—a festal robe; " girt about the
paps with a golden girdle "—for rest and
festivity, not about the loins, as in war
and labor. " His head and his hair were
white like wool, as white as snow "—not
the sign of old age, but of purity and
glory, as preintimated when transfigured,
when his "garments became white and
glistering ; " " his eyes were as a flame

of fire "—glowed with pureness and sincerity; " his feet like unto fine brass, as if they burned in a furnace "—brightness and splendor, a furnace aglow, a molten motion, moving in holiness ; " his voice as the sound of many waters "—the majesty of the ocean when the sound is heard from the responsive shore. " His countenance was as the sun shineth in his strength "—like the noontide glory of the sun in a cloudless sky. " Out of his mouth went a sharp two-edged sword "—the law and the Gospel, justice and mercy. " He had in his right hand seven stars "—the seven ministers of the seven churches of Asia under his protecting care. " And when I saw him, I fell at his feet as dead "—no wonder; such would have been the effect upon

us. " He laid his right hand upon me "—
how like the gentle Christ—and said:
" Fear not "—it is the old assurance, " It
is I; be not afraid"—"I am he that was
dead "—you remember my death and
burial; " behold, I am alive for evermore "—immortal fact; and have the
keys of hell and of death "—all authority
over all departed spirits.

How different this personal appearance of Christ as St. John's friend, and
his official appearance as seen at a subsequent period, as " King of kings, and
Lord of lords," on a " white horse "—
symbol of triumph. " His eyes were as
a flame of fire, and on his head were many
crowns "—tokens of his sovereignty.
"He was clothed with a vestment dipped
in blood "—significant of the atonement;

"and his name is called The Word of God"—indicative that he conquers the world by moral forces.

We found the monks of Patmos familiar with the beautiful legends of St. John's life, many of which are in a volume in the library of the monastery, not a few of which rest on strong probability. Whether the release of the apostle came in the reign of Vespasian or at the beginning of that of his son Titus, there is a general agreement that he returned to Ephesus and resumed the personal oversight of the seven churches of Ionic Asia. His return was a jubilee to the Christians and a renewed assurance that Christ was walking among the golden candlesticks. As the islands of the Levant were then thickly populated and

Patmos is not more than twenty-five miles from Samos, marking the ancient port of Ephesus, it is supposable that St. John had been kept informed as to the great events which were occurring throughout the Roman empire ; that he knew when Nero committed suicide and the throne was left to Vespasian ; when Jerusalem was destroyed, and when Titus became master of the Roman world. Nor was he uninformed as to the progress of Christianity both east and west, and especially as to the spiritual conditions of the Asian churches.

More than twenty years of his life are yet before him to confirm the believer, to combat the heretic, to overthrow pagan Rome. He is now an itinerant, and goes from Ephesus to Smyrna, through the valley of the Cayster and the Hermus, where he visits Polycarp, bishop of that renowned city; thence sixty miles to Pergamos, on the river Cetius, built of white marble, where stood a temple to Æsculapius, and where "Antipas, my faithful martyr, was slain;" thence fifty miles to Thyatira, on the banks of the Caicus, where that "woman Jezebel" had seduced the people. Continuing his journey, he came to Sardis, situated on the river Pactolus, that great and prosperous city, once the proud capital of Lydia, the pride of Crœsus, where were "a few names even in Sardis which have not defiled their garments; and they shall walk with me in white: for they are worthy." Threading his way along the valley of the Hermus, he comes to Philadelphia, which has survived all the revolutions of time— " Because thou hast kept the word of my patience, I also will keep thee from the hour of temptation ;" and following the rocky paths along the slopes of Mount Tmolus, he arrives at Laodicea, rich and grand, whose believers were " neither cold nor hot."

But Ephesus was his metropolitan city, whose careless Christians had " left their first love," and where resided those professed believers who denied our Lord's human nature, who asserted that his body was a mere appearance without substance or reality. While there he has the pen of a ready writer and com- pletes the sacred canon of the New Tes- tament, to supply what Matthew, Mark, and Luke had omitted, and to refute certain errors there rife and give to the Church and the world a larger view of Christ.   There St. John writes his gospel, the most precious of all the Holy Scriptures.   It is a clear, calm, courageous declaration of the two natures of Christ, " God manifest in the flesh," a revelation to the world of Christ as St. John knew and saw and realized him in his personal experience; it is the opening of the divine heart of Jesus to the gaze of the world. Of the eight miracles he records, six are new and such as to convince men that they might believe in Jesus and " have life through his name." It is the most powerful and overwhelming attestation of the truth of Christianity extant; and because of this inherent

power on the intellect and over the con-
science of the world it has been assailed
by a bitterness of opposition not expressed against either of the other gospels. It is the recorded testimony of
an eye witness himself who suffered all
things for the truth.

The monks of Patmos could add little
to the accepted legends touching the
closing scenes in the life of this illustrious man, and referred us to the early
fathers, who collated and transmitted
those occurrent events in his private life
and public ministry which have come
to us, and which make so attractive the
biographies of great men. This is the
charm of Plutarch's Lives of those renowned Greeks and Romans of whom
we never weary reading, when related

by such a master hand.   Much he writes
is legendary, yet his legends have the
flavor of truth and high probability.
From Polycarp, St. John's friend and
disciple, down to the historian Eusebius,
there was a succession of bishops, who
recorded what they had known and heard
of the " Beloved Disciple," and their record is true.   The story of the partridge
tamed and caressed by St. John, with
which he played to relieve the tension
of mental strain, is not unworthy an
apostle ; it is the old story of the hunt-
er's unbent bow.   That he was ship-
wrecked when on his way from Palestine to Ephesus is in keeping with the
checkered life of the Lord's chosen
friends, who are not exempt from the
ills which befall less honored men.   His

pursuit of the young robber to the far-off mountains of Pergamos, the resort of thieves, to rescue from a life of sin and shame one who had fallen away during John's exile, is so Christlike and beautiful as to make it a reality. The resurrection of the good Drusiana finds a parallel in the restoration to life of Tabitha of Joppa by St. Peter. This holy woman of Ephesus excelled in all good works, and her home had been the home of the apostle. On the day of his return from Patmos he met her funeral procession, and, approaching the bier, he prayed and his friend returned to life. Such was the sanctity of his person and the protecting care heaven had over him, that no harm came to him when compelled to drink from the poisoned cup;

that no rain fell on the uncovered oratory where he preached in Ephesus, and wherein he wrote his gospel and his three epistles; that when he felt his end approaching he had his grave prepared, and calmly laid himself down therein to die; and that his sepulcher in Mount Prion was known to Polycarp and Ignatius and Papias, who were with him to the last.

Poetry and art have rescued him from the grave and given a legendary interpretation to the Saviour's words, " If I will that he tarry till I come, what is that to thee?" In a splendid work on sacred and legendary art there is a story worthy of immortality: " King Edward the Confessor had a special veneration for St. John. One day, returning from his church at Westminster, where he had been hearing mass in honor of the evangelist, he was accosted by a pilgrim, who asked him for an alms for the love of God and St. John. The king drew from his finger a ring, and, unknown to anyone, gave it to the beggar. When the king had reigned twenty-four years, two pilgrims, Englishmen, in the Holy Land, who were about to return to England, were met by one who was also in the habit of a pilgrim, who inquired of what country they were ; and, on being told of England, he said to them, 'When ye shall have arrived in your own country, go to King Edward and salute him in my name. Say to him that I thank him for the alms bestowed on me in a certain street in Westminster; for there on a certain day, as I begged of him an alms, he bestowed on me this ring. And ye shall carry it back to him, saying that in six months from this time he shall quit the world and come and remain with me forever.'

"The pilgrims, being astonished, said, 'Who art thou, and where is thy dwelling place?' And he, answering, said, 'I am John the Evangelist; Edward, your king, is my friend, and for the sanctity of his life I hold him dear. Go now, therefore, deliver him this message and this ring, and I will pray to God that ye may arrive safely in your own country.' He then vanished out of their sight.

"The pilgrims, praising and thanking the Lord for this vision, went on their journey. Arrived in England, they repaired to the king and delivered the ring and message. The king received the news joyfully, conferred honors on the pilgrims, and prepared himself to depart according to the message he had received."